The End of Everything
and
Everything That Comes after That

WISCONSIN POETRY SERIES

Sean Bishop and Jesse Lee Kercheval, *series editors*
Ronald Wallace, *founding series editor*

The End of Everything

and

Everything That Comes after That

NICK LANTZ

THE UNIVERSITY OF WISCONSIN PRESS

Publication of this book has been made possible, in part, through support from the Brittingham Trust.

The University of Wisconsin Press
728 State Street, Suite 443
Madison, Wisconsin 53706
uwpress.wisc.edu

Gray's Inn House, 127 Clerkenwell Road
London EC1R 5DB, United Kingdom
eurospanbookstore.com

Printed in the United States of America
This book may be available in a digital edition.

Library of Congress Cataloging-in-Publication Data

Names: Lantz, Nick, author.
Title: The end of everything and everything that comes after that / Nick Lantz.
Other titles: Wisconsin poetry series.
Description: Madison : The University of Wisconsin Press, 2024. |
Series: Wisconsin poetry series
Identifiers: LCCN 2023040938 | ISBN 9780299347949 (paperback)
Subjects: LCGFT: Poetry.
Classification: LCC PS3612.A586 E53 2024 | DDC 811/.6—dc23/eng/20231010
LC record available at https://lccn.loc.gov/2023040938

For Vicky

Contents

1

Ruin   3

Poem on a Photo of a Reflection of a Bowl of Plastic Fruit   5

A Bow, a Basket, a Cloud   7

Poem Not Ending with a Phone Call   9

The Rabbit   12

Poem Not Ending with a Gesture   14

After Aeschylus   16

Poem Not Ending with U.S. Border Agents Tear-Gassing
    Migrant Children   22

I Feel Like a Million $ 23

Poem Not Ending with Francisco Vázquez de Coronado   25

The Three Types of Knowledge   27

Poem Not Ending in a Shrug   29

2

Word of the Day   33

Word of the Day   34

Word of the Day   35

Word of the Day   36

Word of the Day   37

Word of the Day	38
Word of the Day	39
Word of the Day	40
Word of the Day	41
Word of the Day	42
Word of the Day	43
Word of the Day	44
Word of the Day	45
Word of the Day	46
Word of the Day	47
Word of the Day	48
Word of the Day	49
Word of the Day	50
Word of the Day	51
Word of the Day	52
Word of the Day	53
Word of the Day	54
Word of the Day	55
Word of the Day	56
Word of the Day	57
Word of the Day	58
Word of the Day	59
Word of the Day	60
Word of the Day	61
Word of the Day	62
Word of the Day	63
Word of the Day	64
Word of the Day	65
Word of the Day	66

Word of the Day   67

Word of the Day   68

Word of the Day   69

3

Postoperative   73

Poem Not Ending with the President's Hands Upturned in an
    Expression of Unfathomable Indifference   74

Poem Not Ending with Anesthesia   75

Ode to the Dead of Bowling Green   77

A Cloud Weighs over a Million Pounds   78

Poem Not Ending with My Grandfather's Will   82

Photograph of My Wife Shaving My Head   84

Mise en Abyme   86

The Survivorship   89

"Terrific," "Tremendous," "Loser," "Tough," "Smart," "Weak,"
    "Dangerous," "Great," "Stupid," "Classy," "Big," "Huge,"
    "Amazing," "Lightweight," "Win," "Bad," "Crooked," "Moron,"
    "We," "They," "Zero"   91

My Father, Singing   92

Poem Not Ending with a Transcript of the Final Voicemails of
    9/11 Victims   94

An Urn for Ashes   96

Acknowledgments   99

I

Ruin

But I am a ruin myself, wandering among ruins.

—HEINRICH HEINE

At Ground Zero, fifteen years later, a bachelor party
    poses for pictures
        with a blow-up sex doll—
meaning, a human mouth pressed itself to a valve,

    and human lungs
        pumped human breath
into that body, breath like wind hissing
    through crumbled masonry.
        Everyone

has a burning building inside them. (Maybe
    just a dollhouse
        smoking from its dormers.
Or a dictator's palace perfumed with jet fuel.)

    The tractors plowing
        the fields around my family's
farmhouse still turn up stone arrowheads.
    It's rare these days
        to find anything other

than a broken point, but I've held one, whole,
    long as my palm and still
        sharp, and I've walked
old midden mounds fenced into cow pastures,

their soft rise like the lump
               my hand finds under
the skin while soaping my body in the shower.
        Life is all gilded frescoes
                       and Arnold Palmers

at the clubhouse until Titus and his men
        pass through with torches,
                       until Cortés and his men
pass through with torches, until Sherman

        and his men and so on,
                until men forget
what their hands looked like without torches.
        In Mosul, men sledgehammer statues
                       millennia older
than the prayers they speak to god, and in the light
        of this century,
                which is the shaky light
thrown by torches, I think prayer is the breath

        blown into some flimsy
                body, its insides
reeking of smoke from the burning buildings
        men carry around inside them
                       (some, whole

tenements howling fire from every window,
        and others only ash.) And how
                in that farmhouse
I loved (which once burned too) a clock

        with arrowheads instead of numbers
                hangs
on the wall, counting down the sharp seconds.

Poem on a Photo of a Reflection of a Bowl of Plastic Fruit

In one of my body's cellular factories
a worker falls asleep, and boom: cancer.
Imagine it like that scene from *I Love Lucy*
with the chocolates piling up so fast
Lucy starts shoving them in her mouth.
Or like the game of telephone kids play:
a sentence goes ear-to-ear-to-ear-etc. but
want comes back *ant*, *bread* goes *dead*.
St. Jerome mistranslates *karan* as *keren*,
so 1,500 years later, Michelangelo
sculpts Moses sporting horns
like a pair of tumors on his forehead.
Say *seventy-seven benevolent elephants*
ten times fast. Or better yet, repeat
the word *cancer* until it's just a shape
the mouth makes, a bee circling
a silk flower. Every day my wife
injects blood thinner into a catheter
in my arm, and when it hits my heart
I taste melted plastic. You can't eat
plastic fruit, but hey, it never rots.
Some forgeries are worth millions,
but when I say *funny*, my students
don't laugh. So here's a joke for you:
"One side effect of chemo is cancer."
Don't even get me started on X-rays,
how just looking for something
enough can conjure it to life. Is that
the same as prayer? Lightning leaves

its glowing imprint on the eye,
my wife's cool handprint remains
on my scalp—if only for a moment.
But that's how I know for sure
that sugar is sweet, because the ant
carries it away grain by stolen grain.

A Bow, a Basket, a Cloud

from Latin, *detonare*, to expend
    thunder, light /

from *sympiptein*, to befall, to coincide,

        the truck and deer meeting on a road,
    cloud-muted moon /

from *malignantem*, to act with ill intent—

        the wounded cloud,
    the crowd seizing forward /

from *kytos*, meaning empty

    container, a basket, the body

        a series of baskets, rickety stack
    against the market wall /

from *arcus*, belonging to the bow, called *toxon*, root
    of *toxic*, Herakles dipping
        his arrows in the hydra's poison blood /

from *bodig*, trunk, structure, principal part /

from *hearm*, pain, grief, insult /

from *methistanai*, to take away, to alter /

five swallows fall dead on the lawn overnight,
                    the morning spent
          examining a cloudless sky /

from *karkinos*, pincered scavenger creeping
          pale as a cloud and hard as stone /

from *ektemnein*, consisting of *ek* (out) + *temnein* (to cut), the latter
                    giving *tome*, single volume excised
          from a multivolume work, body
of work, the body as work, ongoing /

from *lapara*, the flank, the tender expanse between rib
          and hip /
from *skopein*, to examine /

from *wyrgan*, to provoke anxiety, to vex, but also
          to strangle /

from *orkhis*, literally *testicle*, root
          of *orchid*, of which there are thirty thousand
     varieties, all fragile, ornamental, foolish /

from *clud*, meaning a stone
          or rock, the latter denoting
                    a formation, the former
          a single object, such as that hurled
through a window reflecting

     only empty sky /

Poem Not Ending
with a Phone Call

The windshield crack starts
            small, the size of a metaphor,
the size of a nonspecific subcentimeter sclerotic lesion
      on the left iliac bone, the size
            of my grandma/colleague/neighbor

in the voting booth making America great again.
      For twenty years, the launch codes
            in the Minuteman silos
were set to zero zero zero zero zero zero zero. True,

      I can't remember the phone number
            for the pink stucco house
where my never-married parents split, but I can feel earthquakes
      shimmying nails out of its walls,
            a fire in the hills

and yellow smoke like a miles-wide comb-over.
      Sonny the auto glass technician
            hooks his finger
under the wiper, says that's how it happens: something

      hits the glass, too small
            to even hear it,
and then the crack starts—like the moment in the phone call
      when I realize you
            are drunk, have been drinking

throughout our conversation, that what I thought
    was breathing was
        swallowing, and you keep sobbing
I'm sorry and *I want to fix you*, by which you mean

    my body, and though the body
        is indeed like glass,
brittle and transparent and visible only when broken,
    there is no fixing it, not really,
        no technician to pry it out

and lower in a pristine replica. Pulling weeds beside the house,
    I get dizzy, and when I lean
        against the siding, the impression
of my hand stays there in wood I now realize is rotten,

    and I think of the man
        who walks his dog in the park
where I walk, how we passed each other three times smiling
    before I noticed his
        BUILD THAT WALL! button. The crack

starts the size of a worm eating a tree that will one day
    drop a dead limb on my roof.
        It starts the size
of a hurricane photographed from space, its center

    puckered like a mouth
        saying the word *huge*.
The crack starts small, the size of the meteor I see
    from my backyard
        after all the power has gone out

in the neighborhood. The state kills people
　　　in my town, a few blocks
　　　　　　from where I'm writing
this line, and though they do it now with a needle,

　　　people still joke
　　　　　about how the lights used to flicker,
how the darkness at their dinner table signified
　　　the departure of another darkness.
　　　　　　　　　But they don't speak

about how the lights come back on, how you must then
　　　go on lifting the gleaming spoon
　　　　　　to your mouth.

The Rabbit

On his deathbed, the dictator
orders the execution
of all the watchmakers.
It's OK to laugh at him,
but he's no different than you
or me. One day, our mothers
also set us down and never
picked us up again, and no one
recovers from being a child,
because a child never thinks
This is the last time I'll wear
these shoes with the red stripe.
Scribes used to scrape the ink
from the page and start over.
And anyone who remembers
the person who remembers
what was first written on the page
has been dead for centuries.
Ninety-three-point-six percent of adulthood
is believing *If I could just have those shoes*
with the red stripe again, I'd be happy.
Sometimes we bulldoze
the ruins of an ancient city
to build a shopping mall.
And sometimes we bulldoze
a shopping mall to make way
for another shopping mall.
When my pocket turns out
empty, I want to curse
the tailor. And why not?

He stitched that little
fold of emptiness that rubs
my thigh all day like a bad
lover. I'm writing this poem
by replacing the poem
that used to be here.
And do you see the pair
of rabbit tracks cutting
across the snow,
and where they stop
in the middle of the field—
the imprint of two wings?

Poem Not Ending with a Gesture

The news like fog so thick I can't see the sign
    WARNING: FOG
           but my neighbor presses
his lips to the gap in our shared fence, whispers,

    All human suffering is 99 percent
           gossip, like the alleged
refugee on his alleged raft in the alleged ocean—I mean,
    what's an ocean, anyway?
           OK.

Later that day, my wife and I watch a documentary,
    a children's TV host
           explaining assassination
to a puppet. But time is not like walking out

    of one neighborhood
           and into another.
It's more like the one two three coats of primer
    that can't quite cover
           the swastika sprayed

on the community center door. I mean, OK,
    the door still works, but—
           It makes me think
of the deer we saw crossing the highway

with an arrow
        straight through its neck.
It looked photoshopped, the way it knelt
        and nibbled some grass
                as if nothing was wrong.

In many optical illusions, background information
        influences our perception
                of the foreground object.

Fish   space   fish   space   fish becomes
        bird   space   bird   space etc. Two faces, a chalice.

A White House attorney touches thumb
        to index, fans out
                the other three fingers, and this
becomes a joke, becomes the sound of men laughing

        as they drive away
                from the burnt corpse
they left hanging in a tree. Does that seem
        melodramatic?
                Well, OK, fine. But more

and more, living in this world feels like being beaten
        to death
                with a feather pillow,
while someone stands around mocking you

for bleeding. *What's wrong with you?* he says.
        Can't you take
                a joke?

After Aeschylus

the eagle, struck
by an arrow,
looks down
& recognizes
its own feathers
fletching the shaft

—AESCHYLUS

i. Photo of Monet's Haystacks with the Back of a Tourist's Head in the Foreground

Who's to say? Some Roman traveler, dead now
thousands of years, carved this in the tomb
of Ramesses VI: "I visited and I did not like anything
except the sarcophagus!" Monet walks into a field
with an easel tucked under his arm, and there goes
the neighborhood. Now, a sorrow of tourists floats
the gallery, snapping blurry pics of haystacks. Meanwhile,
the office park's Bucolic Brook™ sounds like god
riffling a stack of twenties, but water recognizes
water, just like Heather in HR sees her own face
catching shafts of sunset in the breakroom poster's
dusty glass, Parsippany's light falling on Giverny's
just so. The calligrapher inks the character for *mouse*
with a mouse-whisker brush. Who are we to complain?
Even the handle of the axe comes from the forest.

ii. Birds of a Feather

Be careful me fine friends, the gods have been angered by
all this celebratin'.

—Michael the Macaw

I'm sweating on a bench in Disney's Enchanted Tiki Room,
thinking about how imagineers programmed the birds' whistle
and clatter with the same tech that ran the Polaris missiles,
weapons designed for their *countervalue*—that is, imagined to unimagine
whole cities. Call it feeble luck that we've survived our own history
so far. But *someone* must build the gallows, we told ourselves
as we put hammer to nail, then put town in our rearview
before the hangings began. Every tool recognizes its duty:
the sheath its complicity, the knife its insight. We're the ones
who pretend, fleshing the past in song and the piped-in scent
of popcorn. Meanwhile, our clockwork cranks itself. The automatic
doors swing wide for the stray dog wandering in from our ruin,
the radioactive dust on his coat an enchantment, his sores
and bleeding gums shiny as our imaginations.

iii. Fifteen Acres

A seer tells King Oleg his horse will kill him, so Oleg
kills the horse. Years later, he comes across its bones
in a field and laughs. *Stupid horse! Dead horse! Ha!*
O, America, I'm tired of personifying you. Take this hill
of ants. This heart like a diesel truck idling in the drive-thru.
This dead guard dog named Pharaoh. Yes, I've studied art—
the politician's textbook frown after every school shooting.
The fires. Even an ant recognizes itself in a mirror, and hell
has its own weather, its own beachfront gift shops
where we smooth our sweaty bills on the counter. The NRA
says its annual convention this year features fifteen acres
of guns. And did you guess how it ends? How Oleg's laughter
echoes like hammers over the fields of his wide domain?
How he kicks the horse's skull? How a snake crawls out?

iv. Cartoon Metaphysics

I dove into a swimming pool of gold coins and broke both legs,
but hey, that's late capitalism for you. So now here I am,
pouring birdseed in the middle of this huge red bull's-eye
painted on the road, expecting—what, exactly? Let's not
speak of the tornado, the steeple plucked from its church,
birds pecking out the scarecrow's straw for their nests. Yes,
I've worn the crooked crown of bluebirds chirping bright
doom, but no one recognizes he's run off the cliff's edge
until he looks down. Better I go on dangling anvils, piling up
TNT, sketching the last outlines of my failure. The first coyote
I ever saw was pawing at cold fries in a parking lot. *Beep beep*
went the cars. And that bull's-eye? It throbs all night long
above the building where my wife and I convince ourselves
that our sadness is the exact size and shape of a credenza.

v. Deer Hoof Gun Rack

*And let it go badly for you, shadows of hell, who devour
all beautiful things.*

—CATULLUS

The old midden mounds are full of fishhooks
carved from the bones of fish, just as shopping malls
are full of old midden mounds and bad analogies.
On further inspection, all the art I've ever loved
boils down to *people suck, but*—
                like Judith's steady
sword hand or the sparrow on Lesbia's lap, the way
its tiny claws hook her gown as it chirps to her.
On your man-cave wall, two upturned hooves recognize
that hell keeps its own ledger of questionable debts,
just as Gentileschi's brush keeps Judith's sword sharp,
just as Catullus's poem holds the dead sparrow,
his lover's grief. I hate to joke of it, but I adore
Catullus's *but*, that curse flung against indifferent
darkness, the shape of a belief, the way the hooves believe
that if they just hold your gun for long enough, one day
you'll take it down from the wall and blow your brains out.

vi. The Waffle House Index

—an informal metric used by FEMA to gauge disaster severity

In ancient Babylon, they tied three answers to three arrows,
and whichever flew farthest told the truth. Today, I shopped
online for face masks for my cats. If Waffle House stays open,
will the armed gunmen parading the capitol fly away like angry
birds? Will the medieval muck serfs walked in stop sticking
to our shoes? Will the wheelbarrow of dead bodies cease
its rattle? The word *we* makes a crooked sound when we
talk disaster, but please recognize that every apocalypse requires
its own measure of ruin. Ours just happens to be pan-fried.
Others read dust, placenta, barley, the melting of wax, needles,
cracks in a burning donkey's skull, comet tails, even—don't laugh—
poetry. The trick is, you only get a stone's answer from a stone.
You shuffled the deck. You ordered hash browns ALL THE WAY.
To the executioner, the word *hope* just sounds like *rope*.

Poem Not Ending
with U.S. Border Agents
Tear-Gassing Migrant Children

. . . it's natural. You could actually put it on your nachos and eat it.

—RON COLBURN, Border Patrol Foundation president

We drowned the witches in triple-distilled spring water. When we cracked the skulls of striking miners, we did it with truncheons carved from the finest old-growth hickory. We lit the inconvenient darkness with our torches. We lotioned our hands before we choked, polished our boots before we kicked. Let no one forget we chartered those thousands of cruises across the Atlantic. The night before the protest, we fed the dogs with diced lamb kidneys. And what is a stone—really, after all—if not a piece of history, formed by millions of years of geology to fit just so in our hands? We can verify the ropes were 100 percent American hemp. When you cried out, we closed our blinds to protect your modesty. The cell was so spotless, you could eat off the floor. The guns were always well oiled. The blankets were incredibly soft.

I Feel Like a Million $

A nickel ain't worth a dime anymore.
                              —YOGI BERRA

I wish I could rub a hundred-dollar bill on my heart
and be cured of sadness, but there's more bacteria
on the average dollar than on a public toilet seat.
Speaking of which, have you ever gone to the movies
and slipped out to the bathroom only to discover
a lump on your testicle, then returned to the theater
and sat beside your wife as if nothing were wrong,
while up on screen a corpse coughed silver coins?
Just me? We live in the country that printed
MIND YOUR BUSINESS on its first penny,
though the mind is a terrible business, all retail therapy
and one-eyed pyramids beaming carcinogenic rays
over the field where children play hide and seek.
Ask the Romans—they'll tell you the end
of civilization is always gold-plated, that the rain
falling soft as singles can't wash away the blood
in the Colosseum. If I ever wondered about the worth
of my life, now I can just count the commas
in my chemo bill, and when that's done, I hold up
every belonging in my house and ask if it sparks
joy—*Can you just spark joy for goddamn once?*—and then
put it back. A waiter pulls what he thinks is a twenty
from under the ketchup bottle, only to discover
it's a pamphlet shouting SOME THINGS ARE BETTER
THEN MONEY! LOVE THE LORD JESUS!
The government is shut down, and Crystal Minton
of Florida is very upset with her president: *I thought
he was going to do good things. He's not hurting
the people he needs to be hurting.* Sometimes love,

any love, feels like throwing good money after bad.
I don't remember what the Louisiana Purchase bought,
but I remember my dad's advice: carry a roll of nickels
in your pocket if you go out drinking, because a hand
wrapped around two hundred grams of metal can break a jaw
like it's nothing. How can I judge Crystal when my fist
is a hardened wad of twenties burning a hole in my pocket
and the world is full of faces I'd love to spend it on?
So, no, you don't have to tell me that *testicular cancer*
is as redundant as *ATM machine*. But it's a funny thing:
when your body's trying to kill you, you still have to take it
to the grocery store to buy lettuce and Windex. You still smile
at the cashier because she's your student, though
you've seen the confederate flag sticker on her truck.
And as you hand her your money, you can wonder
at how so much of civilization depends on knowing
so little about what other people are thinking,
so that when she smiles and says, *Here's your change. Have
a blessed day*, you smile and say *Thank you* and mean it.

Poem Not Ending
with Francisco Vázquez de Coronado

It's a boy!
    —Sonic Boom Exploding Target Gender Reveal Kit

From a long way off, I see it: not my body: smoke rising
from where my body must be: an indexical sign: the bits
of stubble I can't seem to wipe from the sink: how we give
names: a city/county/state for the people we displaced:
not erased, quite: obscured: refraction of causation: so often
the law creates the crime: ergo, I cut off the snake's head
with a shovel before checking whether it's poisonous:
what I see in myself being what I see in others: a false
cognate: the hot-pink AR-15 kit, the personal sanitary wipes
packaged in black: FOR MEN: capital letters like a fence:
a border, even: so you are not confused: the law is clear:
the gun under his jacket: licensed, legal, as opposed to:
the My Kitty Self-Defense Keychain in your pocket:
a class-A misdemeanor, up to one year in jail, a $4,000 fine,
or both: a redundancy: e.g., final outcome, armed gunman,
fatigue-green bath bomb shaped like a grenade: but we joke:
we know the difference: the pink ALLERGIC 2 ALGEBRA shirt
vs. the man who bashes in a jogger's head because she won't
smile at him: we say, *One more cigarette won't kill me* or *My best friend
wasn't raped because I laughed at that joke in high school*: the slope
is too slippery for us: for me: the icebergs sweat while I cut up
plastic pop bottle rings: it's like trying to grab a handful
of smoke: like Coronado blundering around the Southwest
looking for the seven cities of gold, killing villagers, falling
from his horse: the forest we name after him near the border
of Arizona and Mexico: a fire there that swallows 47,000 acres:
the cause: a border patrol agent's gender-reveal party

for his unborn child: an exploding target that, when shot,
plumes blue or pink smoke but also ignites the underbrush:
that smoke—sour and gray and rising for miles—
makes its own declarations: to be a man is to smell
of gunpowder: the way my fingers leave behind the soot
of torches on anything I touch: you can try to interpret
such smudged arcana, look for effect, cause: most of us
just stand in the ashes and shrug and say *What fire?*

The Three Types of Knowledge

My mother says her mother is entering her *end of life*,
to which I say, *Technically, we are all in our end of life*,
to which my mother says, *You should write a poem
about that*, but instead I keep trying to write a poem
about the Mars Curiosity Rover, the engineers
who taught it to hum "Happy Birthday" to itself.
Late at night, I text my mother, tell her to stop
answering those random questions on Facebook.
What was your first pet, and what was its name?
asks Tri-City Lawn Pros above a cartoon dog
in a party hat. *Those are password security questions*,
I say. She responds with videos of hummingbirds
pulsing around her feeder, photos of the occasional
jeweled dead she finds below the kitchen window.
Here's the thing: the rover never sang a second time.
There's no scientific value in its song, and singing
brings its battery closer to death, the same way
when I visit my grandmother in the rehab center
and see in its garden a sign that says SOMETIMES,
I WET MY PLANTS, I also inch incrementally closer
to death. What I really needed to tell you about
is the drive my mother takes between her home
and the rehab center, an hour of cornfields broken
only by Trump signs, but in one pasture a farmer
has erected a sign that says BLACK LIVES MATTER,
and my mother, driving daily into the end
of her mother's life, tells me this sign gives her
some measure of comfort, knowing at least one
other person thinks and feels the way she does,
which is what I always thought a poem did,

a way of knowing you aren't humming
"Happy Birthday" to yourself on a remote planet.
When I visit her and we make the drive
to the rehab center, she slows, says, *Here it comes*,
tapping on the window glass with her nail,
and I get out my camera and take a picture,
the sign black and white against the unforgiving
green of the corn and soybeans. Later, I hold
my grandmother's hand. I sit with her and say
how proud I am when she walks down the hallway
and back again. It is almost her ninety-second birthday.
When I'm back home, my mother texts me at 6 a.m.:
What are the images of the three types of knowledge?
I scroll back through photos she's texted me:
a nail in a tire, her new collapsible ladder,
vultures on the barn roof (*A committee of vultures*, she says).
Only later does she write to say that this is the question
her mother asked, waking from a morphined stupor.
You should answer her question in a poem, she says.
And that's where I'd like to end, but I have to tell you
the truth: when I was in the car with my mother,
I looked at the photograph I'd taken and saw the sign
actually said BLACK CALVES MATTER, and I considered,
for a moment, deleting the photo, not telling my mother,
letting her go on believing what her eyes and heart
had tricked her into seeing, but I didn't, friend,
I told her, just like I'm telling you now.

Poem Not Ending in a Shrug

Letters have fallen off
the local pawn shop sign:
WE B   GOLD
And I want to be gold—
really, I do, but instead
I've learned
how to type
¯_(ツ)_/¯
on my phone.
Let's face it: if you told me
a Texas congressman
tweeted *COVID infects*
wind turbines, which cause abortions
I wouldn't *not* believe you,
but every time I type
¯_(ツ)_/¯
I want to throw my phone
into any of the new lakes
brimmed full by the third
hundred-year-flood
this month. I don't mean
to get off track, but I spent
decades believing
my body was a ship
just chugging along
the empty sea,
when really it was the tip
of an iceberg signing its name
across every passing hull.
But don't worry, the icebergs

are mostly all melted anyway,
and there's always a chance
the melting ice will free
some long-lost alien craft
whose crew will resume
their millennia-old mission
of scrubbing humans
from the planet
like black mold
from under the sink, and maybe
from low-earth orbit
they'll use their ray guns
to carve a giant
¯_(ツ)_/¯
across North America.
Is that too much to ask?
You might think
I'm exaggerating,
but even the sidewalk
is giving me grief:
just this morning,
while waiting to cross
the street, I looked down,
and the concrete asked
    Y U
and my vision blurred
a little, and my chest
felt light, and I stumbled
through the rest of my day
mumbling to myself
Why me? Why me? Why me?

2

Word of the Day

it's Blursday (again) and I'd rather be anything
but awake the wasps in the roof purr their voices
the color of the blood in the toilet bowl I don't
want to alarm you tell me about your mother early
in AA how you'd sneak sips from her water
just to check how you wanted to be right
and to be wrong we swab around our noses
drip the reagent wait for one line or two the other
day walking into Home Depot a guy waved
said good morning young man I am old enough
to be a grandfather I tell you we stare at the dead
cockroaches in your office ceiling light
while we wait for nothing later I pass a woman
lying on the sidewalk hello she blinks at the sun
I uncover my face I just need a minute I need

Word of the Day

how will pizza rat get his pizza while restaurants
are shut down I count fifteen no eighteen deer
in my front yard a doe is nursing a fawn in the middle
of the street in Los Angeles eighth graders return
to school to find a coyote on top of the bookshelf
in the classroom the scientists are calling this
anthropause I get it I turn around for one second
and armadillos have dug up my front lawn rain
has washed away the flagstone path to my door
we're the bad dream the world is trying
to wake from a nightmare I keep having
involves a house and a key that turns
to dust in its lock this is real after work
we pass the corner gas station we see a dead
horse belly up by the pumps by the time
we get home we've forgotten all about it

Word of the Day

the pollen falls so heavy from the trees the stray
cats napping on the patio are coated in golden
dust they leave behind cat-shaped outlines
when they dash off at the sound of the neighbor's dog
on the interstate the sky to the south is dark with rain
the sky to the north dark with smoke so much depends
on where you're looking none of the pumps
at the gas station are working the attendant is cursing
and crying hey says a woman it's OK she says
and I swear someone else is crying a little the nozzle
in his hand suspended like some ugly hummingbird
about to dip its beak into an ugly flower on the hill
below us a construction crew is digging a trench
they've dug it before but they leave it too long and it fills
in this is the third time they've dug it out this year

Word of the Day

eating my sandwich outside I think a bird
lands on my shoulder it's a face mask
I block the same number again and again
but I keep getting the same call telling me
America is wounded will I stop the bleeding
will I commit my twenty dollars cut it out
says the surgeon the radiation oncologist
says only a little will get into your brain
says imagine a sunburn about the size
of a quarter the surgeon says he'll take
a bit of skin from my chest the bird
goes skipping across the parking lot

Word of the Day

a voice outside a locked door keeps saying come look
at my badge bro and did you know the snow falling
on Dorothy and her friends in that poppy field
was asbestos my mom says dying involves a lot
of paperwork we only got twenty copies of Dad's
death certificate she says but we needed more we'll get
more for Mom just to be safe we're not taking
that risk say the teens huddled in the locked
classroom to the voice who may be a deputy
or may be their classmate who's just murdered
three other classmates with a gun his father
bought on Black Friday spiders it turns out also suffer
from arachnophobia they know to fear predator species
they've never encountered before bro says the voice
on the last day of classes only half my students
show up we all repeat a line from a Mary Ruefle poem
over and over again around the room someone
stops at the window looking in watching us

Word of the Day

the hosts of the true crime podcast somehow always
playing in my house like to say full-body chills like to say
preparanoid like to say you never know and trust your
intuition the man from across the street tells me
and my wife about a murder from many years ago
a man who [   ] a nine-year-old girl in the head
while forcing her to [   ] on him while we stand
arms full of heavy boxes he rambles his retirement
the Title IX case against him all nonsense of course
he would never say anything inappropriate
to a colleague never I shouldn't have told you that
the looks on our faces except we're wearing masks
the dog in the yard north of us barks at the dog
in the yard south of us this goes on for a hundred years

Word of the Day

my mother texts me while I'm explaining a poem
to my students the idea of a turn my mother texts
me at the mechanic while I wait for the headlight
replacement the pillow pitchman on TV complaining
about being canceled my mother texts me a picture
of my grandmother dying she's peaceful says
my mother inside my mask I breathe her oxygen
levels keep dropping texts my mother here's the rose
the hospice nurse dropped off the sneering pundit
pretends to care about migrant children moments
before she cuts to the reporter aboard the new
border patrol helicopter what do you think
she says a real force multiplier he says gesturing
at the desert below him I breathe in the margin
of a student's poem I write have you considered
how nostalgia can be a kind of poison my mother
texts me again the Italian word is volta the moment
when my hand drifts to my pocket after a phantom
buzz like a shivering animal against my thigh
there's nothing this time this time I imagined it

Word of the Day

I used to think the end of the world was the worst
thing that could happen now I worry what if this
world doesn't end I realized I often don't finish
reading the books I love I lay them face down
their words against the table or my thigh it's easy
to do nothing it's easy to stay busy but time
is a shovel digging up a mass grave and you
keep telling yourself surely it will run out of bones
but here's the thing it won't they should ban
high-capacity magazines says my mother
every reasonable person has a reasonable solution
they can scream at everyone else but take it
from a poet you can't carry water in a sentence
a poem can't hold moonlight as it falls the broken
arches of ruins used to frighten me but yesterday
I read it only takes a few minutes for a gun barrel
to cool completely I wish I could promise you
ruins but I opened the curtains this morning
and the street was still there cars headed to

Word of the Day

a truck carrying a hundred monkeys has crashed
in Pennsylvania and at least three monkeys
escaped well good for them my neighbor won't
take down her Christmas lights I need this
she says Mt. Everest gets taller every year
I still remember the student who walked
in and blurted out y'all what is the moon
when I can't sleep at night I paint miniature
plastic zombies with a brush fine as a needle
look at their little faces sagged with hunger
I use a magnifying glass to get the hollow
of their eyes the right kind of empty
in the waiting room I can't concentrate
on the forms I'm supposed to fill out
what surgery what year I keep listening to
the woman on her phone saying my dear
my dear my dear my dear my dear

Word of the Day

the day before my surgery Facebook offers me
a photo collage celebrating my thirteen years
of friendship with a friend who died ten years
ago of the same cancer I got nine years ago
sometimes I think my phone is listening to me
I say something to my wife about lizards
and just like that ads for terrarium decorations
start appearing in my feeds fake log fake
pirate ship crickets delivered live to your door
my friend who died was born on the same day
as me same year I walk out of this newest
surgery with my head wrapped in gauze
like some old-timey toothache I realize
I forgot to tell my dad I was even having
surgery which is odd because I've always
worried he'll die and I won't find out
till months later his brother died that way
half-melted into a couch before anyone
noticed the smell no one noticed my friend
was dying actually we noticed the weight loss
the way he'd nod off while talking but we believed
him when he said his test results were clear
that he was still driving to his job every morning
and not to idle in a mall parking lot that he just
wasn't hungry and at his wedding when he almost
collapsed I caught him his body lighter than
a child's and I put him in a chair and brought him
a glass of coke because I was a good friend

Word of the Day

I know I know I probably shouldn't but I leave out
food for the stray cats they've learned to gather
at the creak of the gate but won't come close
to me my mother is drafting her holiday card
on a sheet of paper towel at the table she's visiting
after her mother's death a canceled trip in the fall
her cards always quote a poem her cards always
arrive late I drive her out to see the historical village
gaze at the deathbed of the very historical person
the pistols given to him by his commanding officer
through Plexiglas you can see a table laid out
with a feast the glossy slices of plastic roast beef
if I'm late to feed the cats they don't complain
they don't complain about the rain the freeze
I see a coyote trotting along the edge of the woods
nosing the ground I hate it when animals appear
prophetically in poems the deer with its wise antlers
the poem in my mother's card is by Mary Oliver
something about joy and grief my doctor shaves
a pea-sized lump off my scalp drops it in a metal
bowl not unlike the ones I leave out for the cats
is that something I should put in a poem my doctor
likes to make guns with his hands and shoot me
with them as if to say bang bang you're dead
he means this in the friendliest possible way
my mother pages through a book of poems says
I can't remember if there's a period after grief

Word of the Day

as the roller coaster drops me into the really
pretty good reproduction of Monument Valley
the lap bar says I won't be flung against
the rocks so OK in Indiana family photos
from a home a hundred miles away settle
like snow on a stranger's lawn in the dark Hall
of Presidents someone shouts Let's go Brandon
the darkness fills with laughter a trick of mirrors
projects a hitchhiking ghost into our carriage
the wildfire stirs its own weather system a woman
points to her basement wall above her head
where the floodwater has marked a line
I pass a hundred no more men who look
exactly like me same sunburn same T-shirt
with a cartoon duck oh but one man's shirt
says I Love One Woman and Many Guns
management told the dead candle factory workers
they'd be fired if they left early to get home
before the tornado hit you can buy candles
scented like the water on the ride with the fake
pirates the ones who have been burning down
the same small village for fifty years

Word of the Day

I read an article called What Your Annoying
Household Habits Say about You I am not
a leave-the-dishes-to-soak person but I abandon
leftovers in the fridge until they're furred
with mold my cousin apparently lets unopened
mail pile up for months he's a doctor you know
an anesthesiologist I wonder if all the doctors
who've put me under leave piles of unpaid bills
on their coffee tables uncashed birthday checks
from their grandmothers who have since died
someone in my building keeps posting flyers
Scientists Are Lying to You about Climate Change
I spend all month pulling them down winter
turns into summer cicadas the size of sparrows
throw themselves at the windows all night
sometimes I can't bear to open the container
of rotten food to throw it away to wash out
the plastic I just toss the sealed container
whole forgive me I've done much worse
I've let people die without telling them
I loved them they went to sleep that final
time and I was thinking about bills I was

Word of the Day

skiers ski down slopes made of forty-two million
cubic feet of artificial snow in a Valentine's card
my mother sends a list of all her accounts
of which I'm the beneficiary just in case she says
my neighbor catches a man sprinkling rat poison
into the bowls she leaves out for feral cats I can't
stop rewatching a video of an Olympian weeping
into a microphone I'm forty years old he says
I'm running out of chances at the zoo fundraiser
you can pay to name a mouse after anyone
you want for an extra fee you get a personalized
video of your mouse being fed to a snake well not
your mouse a frozen mouse the zoo is very clear
they don't feed live mice to snakes the little frozen
mouse died somewhere else don't worry about it

Word of the Day

I'm reading about how the rehearsal of the fake
shooting became a real shooting I'm lying
on a gurney killing time trying to slow
my heart rate the nurse asks the man in the next bed
if he smokes yes if he drinks no if he's pregnant
we have to ask can you believe it I can hear him
shaking his head through the thin curtain
that divides us I'm guessing more than that divides
us a poet I respected wrote an essay about dying
of cancer in the same hospital where I was treated
for cancer I recognized the fish tanks he described
in its lobbies we're all equal in the kingdom of cancer
he said but we aren't I wanted to tell him but then
he was dead I'm reading about the smirking
teenage gunman the judge who has forbidden
the prosecution from calling his victims victims
the nurse makes small talk sticks me one two three
I lose count times looking for a vein in mythology
sleep and death are often related but I imagine
death is closer to general anesthesia where you don't
dream I watch the anesthesiologist's thumb
on the plunger while Living on a Prayer plays
from the radio the doctor tells the nurse
there are twenty-five languages in Guatemala
some of them don't even speak Spanish he says
huh she says huh and then someone is waking
me up handing me a sheet of photographs
of my insides the caverns of my body these could be
anyone's insides but I know they're mine even though
it'll be a few more seconds yet before I can remember
exactly which one of these people I am supposed to be

Word of the Day

I'm done with it says the student on her cell phone
in the parking lot grackles are probably the most
aptly named animal except maybe the slug or
the cockroach it's easier to name something ugly
I wake up and my ear is full of wax huh I say
when my wife asks how my classes went the truth
is sometimes I pretend not to hear to make a point
when she's shouting from the living room
and I'm in the kitchen washing dishes and she
is watching TV and I am watching TV louder
to not hear her TV show I do sometimes wish
little songbirds would land on my outstretched
finger but instead an ant bites me and I have to
Vaseline off my wedding band before my hand
swells up the truth is sometimes I pretend
not to hear because I love the sound of her
voice and I want to hear her say it again huh

Word of the Day

it takes a couple days before I can bring myself
to touch the wound with my bare fingers no piece
of gauze between me and sutures it's alarming
how little it hurts the pain is deeper behind my eye
parts of me where I can't touch Ukraine says
its citizens won't be required to declare seized
Russian military vehicles on their taxes well that's
something my wife says I should make a list
of the parts of my body that have been cut
away but it's not that many really wisdom teeth
a testicle two toenails maybe a half-dozen
lumps of flesh most of which were false
alarms a few that weren't at home I scrub off
the dotted borderline of the skin graft the surgeon
marked on my chest but didn't take gas prices
are up the local gun shops are advertising blowout
sales TikTok is down when I was being stitched
back together I couldn't feel it just a tug
the scrape of a needle while a country song
played over the operating room speakers

Word of the Day

driving to work we ooh and aah at the little baby
horses all shaky-legged in the field I make a joke
about how my mother taps the passenger window
whenever we drive past horses an unusual house
a peach stand in truth OK she did this maybe once
or twice but how can I begrudge it I spend an entire
afternoon answering student emails on the drive home
traffic is stopped a man has punched a mailbox
we inch past the scene the man already in cuffs
a smear of blood on the metal above the address
the little red flag still up all night the campus safety
alert system alerts us a dorm room robbery a rape
stolen spark plugs the suspect descriptions vague
but familiar a famous boxer now mayor posts a video
on Twitter of bodies found shot dead in a ditch this
is genocide he says over the weekend an actor slaps
another actor on TV I'm so happy to be so angry
about something that matters so little wildflowers
spring up overnight or they were always there
but I didn't notice them until we drive back
to work the next day I take a photo but it's blurry

Word of the Day

my feet have gone numb but the cat is sleeping
across my ankles so I don't move I have this problem
ever since chemotherapy where I'm holding a book
and my hands go dead the feeling won't come
back for hours the first time it happened I didn't know
it would ever return I paced the house swinging
my arms flexing my fingers I was alone it was late
at night I thought I might be dying I thought that's
a ridiculous thought to have I drove myself
to the hospital and parked by the glow of the ER doors
I dialed the twenty-four-hour nurse hotline on the back
of my insurance card today at lunch my friends
described the plans they've made if their daughter
ever needs an abortion the distance they'll need
to travel the funds they're setting aside they know
not to text anyone about it not to google the word
even that can be used as evidence it's just a family
vacation to Vancouver they've actually always
wanted to go to Vancouver it's nice there I say
I don't know what to say at night the light catches
on the rain-washed glass of the skyline it's nice

Word of the Day

the sound of children screaming has been removed
says the note preceding the surveillance video do you
remember killer bees or Y2K every morning the same
stray cat returns to my porch with a fresh wound to lick
I remember road rage and stranger danger and needles
slipped into candy bars and Red Asphalt and autopsy
photos of smokers' lungs and the vial of supposedly
crack cocaine the DARE officer let us each hold
briefly in sixth grade you can probably see where
this is headed well none of it got me not the holes
in the ozone layer not acid rain I saw a dog fall out
of a pickup truck on I-5 I didn't sleep for a week
I wouldn't say I walked out of childhood unscathed
but I walked out of it then the new century began
with people falling out of the sky and a city covered
in ash I'm watching an officer in tactical gear pumping
out hand sanitizer from a dispenser in the school
hallway the century is still so incredibly young

Word of the Day

I get emails all the time for other Nick Lantzes
with similar email addresses one is buying
a very expensive house in New Zealand one
is getting custom rims on his truck in Nevada
one in Ohio is a paranormal investigator no joke
I bought ten bags of mulch today but the clerk
charged me for one hundred we had a good
laugh about it the ants are back in the kitchen
I swear I recognize every one of their pinched
faces as they march in under the door a tragedy
fits easily inside a glovebox a purse a drawer
I'm convinced the post office just leaves the flag
at half-mast these days but someone on Twitter
says that not all suffering needs to be poeticized
once a woman emailed me thinking I was her
son she described her hysterectomy asked how
I was doing I wrote back to say I'm not
who you think I am she didn't believe me stop
joking around she said you're not being funny

Word of the Day

so a jockey died on his horse but still won the race
I can't decide if that's a testament to the perseverance
of the horse or the irrelevance of the jockey but I'm sure
it means something like how for the past three years
I've been walking around reading time through a cracked
watch face or the fact frogs use their eyes to help
them swallow or the way the woodpecker wraps
its long tongue around its brain as it bashes its head
against the tree outside my office window bad news
leaks like an old faucet you get used to the sound
of water dripping you can get used to anything but
I can't decide if that's a testament to our resilience
or our weakness those words probably don't matter
there's a tornado watch today which is better
than a warning since a warning often comes too late
my student storms into class she's been crying
she says she's about ready to flip a table I say do it

Word of the Day

campus is closed for a power outage campus
is closed for icy roads the new system update
locked everyone out of their computers I take
a walk I keep lapping the same man he's old
I mean I'm old but he's twice my age easy
he makes a joke each time I pass him making
me look bad he says oh it's you again fancy
seeing you here I nod I wave I stop to read
an article how to spot counterfeit N95 masks
a student sends me an email a photo attachment
he ordered a novel for my class but received
an engineering booklet wrapped in a photocopy
of the novel's cover how to engage the lateral
valve something something can you believe
this says the student I pass the other walker
again his name is Stan he stops me to talk
about the marathons he used to run his heart
attack the device now implanted in his chest
a pacemaker a port for medicine it's unclear
feel it he says taking me by the wrist touching
my hand to the hard plastic under his shirt

Word of the Day

a court just ruled that Pablo Escobar's cocaine hippos
are people protected under the law yesterday I saw
five swans walking out of the woods near my house
to be clear I live in east Texas to be clear I'm not
surprised by much anymore I woke and saw a woman
in the doorway of my bedroom holding something
heavy it was a dream but at the time I thought sure
all right OK can I hold that for you the toilet aboard
the space station is broken the astronauts will spend
most of their two-hundred-day mission in diapers one astronaut
described the situation as suboptimal the thing is
the court has no jurisdiction over the hippos they're in
another country another continent but then again
my neighbor and I live in different realities altogether
he says why are you still wearing that he points
at my face it's not real did you know you can buy
a thong for your iPhone you can buy a $425 capsule
that will make you shit actual gold the most unreal
thing is the suffering you accept without flinching
its great white wings folded as it waddles toward you

Word of the Day

I save a mouse from the cats they only know
how to maim not kill I trap the mouse carry it
outside we're eating sandwiches in a restaurant
when a truck hits a man walking on the side
of the freeway our water heater splits and leaks
like a blister on the news a woman holds
a carrot that grew through a gold wedding band
her grandmother lost in garden dirt forty years
ago the mouse is back in the kitchen soft gray
panic pressed against the baseboard my mother
used to flush them live down the toilet my father
killed them with one swift blow I think about
how all the time radiation from deep space
passes invisibly through us I learn in class
that my twelve students have walked away
from nineteen car accidents maybe it's not
the same mouse I tell myself as I carry it
outside again this time deeper into the woods

Word of the Day

there's nothing quite like the jazzy dance of lawn sprinklers
during a drought I just let the lawn die but I'm indifferent
not principled tourists keep chipping souvenir flecks
off the pyramid or carving their initials in the death camp
bunk beds the dog in the yard next door hates cats and cars
and clouds and the laughter of children the whole crooked
world is rigged against him and he keeps barking terrible
he says terrible terrible in my favorite dystopian film based
on an online quiz based on a fragrance the pink teenage
heroes make out in the car of a defunct roller coaster
while hordes of zombies sway below them like water
I took a one-day falconry course the guide said
training raptors is 90 percent weight management
she took my hand and guided my fingers into the soft
feathers of the horned owl the breastbone is called
the keel it should feel a little sharp if the bird is too fat
the keel dulls and only a hungry bird will fly back to you

Word of the Day

I was reading about aphantasia the inability
to generate mental images though the word
means without imagination a man received
a box full of live iguanas he didn't order
apparently live animals are often misdelivered
says the nonprofit who took the lizards in
a man marched into Burger King with a gun
and declared Trump President King a man
harvesting pine nuts in a hydrogen balloon
came untethered and drifted two hundred miles
before being rescued researchers exhumed
a fifty-five-thousand-year-old mummified bison
and then ate some of its meat so what I'm saying
is imagination is maybe overrated or at least
I wish sometimes my mind was blank
as gray beach sand but see I can't imagine
emptiness without imagining something
empty a box once full of lizards or maybe
a sinkhole that opens up in the street

Word of the Day

while I'm working in my office the custodian puts down
a fresh layer of wax on the hallway floor so I can't leave
I read an article about an artist who wanted to make
a sculpture out of smoke I think about my mother's
collection of abandoned bird nests how some contained
tufts of animal fur or green plastic twine on Friday
a stray cat moved her litter of six kittens under my porch
I bought food and borrowed a trap but Sunday it rained
and Monday they were gone more than once as a kid
I pissed myself in class because I was scared to ask
for a hall pass I read about how the artist died
falling thirty-three stories her husband said she went out
the window he was acquitted but we all know the truth
a deer and her fawn were killed by a car and for days
everyone drove around them meanwhile the fawn's twin
lay curled safe but starving in the grass a hundred feet
away it's hard to blame people for losing interest
in a war you can get an app that will replace every image
of [   ] that comes up in your browser with a picture
of a balloon or a puppy or whatever you want when I leave
my office I see someone walked through the wax
before it dried their footprints go right past the sign
that says NO ENTRY FRESH WAX I put the trap out anyway
bait it with food but I don't catch anything

Word of the Day

at the Renaissance Festival a medieval Batman
and a woman dressed as Spock are eating roast
turkey legs by the axe-throwing booth I've been sick
a week and can't hear out of my right ear to be honest
I don't mind the world a little quieter a little smaller
officials have created a unit to measure the weight
a single byte of information adds to a cell phone
hundreds of sheep in China have been walking
in a circle for days without stopping my wife and I
sit in the stands and cheer the knight from Spain
as he skewers rings on his lance huzzah huzzah
the former president announces his candidacy
the virus is onto sub-sub-sub-variants and someone
bought the dead tech mogul's old sandals
for over two hundred thousand dollars we walk
to the back of the fairgrounds where two elephants
pace a dirt lot covered in straw they're taller
and sadder looking every year and I'm thinking
about the moment the exterminator was getting ready
to spray the baseboards and his wife called him
to say she planned to kill herself my head is full
I almost walk right into the pretzel salesman my wife says
something I say sorry the dragon she says and points
to a girl in a dragon costume marching down
the thoroughfare her little brother holding up her tail

Word of the Day

the wind blurs the sky writer's gauzy letters so that
JESUS SAVES looks to Jessica like her name
the woman I'm walking toward seems to be kissing
a wound on her shoulder but when I pass her by
I see it's a long green lizard tucked into her jacket
I've listened to enough true crime podcasts to know
that people who stumble upon bodies in the woods
often mistake them for mannequins when I was a kid
police came to tell the neighbor about her son and
as they pulled up to the curb she said no dropped
the garden hose walked inside locked the door
the pilot on the intercom keeps pretending to forget
our destination Vegas Acapulco Saskatoon
if you never leave the hotel what difference does it
make in the happiest place on earth a woman
slaps her child so hard the passing crowd all turn
our heads my wife on her walk texts me photos
of police divers in SCUBA gear bobbing in the lake
she asks is it practice or is there a body down there

Word of the Day

the animatronic bear sings with the voice of a man
dead half a century how long is forever how soon
is now or never inflatable lawn decorations rise up
from our neighbors' yard every season yesterday
a pumpkin three ghosts a cat today a pilgrim turkey
leaning on its side the newest shooting is on the news
tonight but a mistake in editing rolls the footage
from last week's shooting instead a server glitch
delivers the same life insurance email to my inbox
over and over again all day the animatronic birds
tell jokes older than me the animatronic president
raises his hand in warning I open a book and out falls
a postcard my mother once sent me she wrote she knew
I'd make the right decision but today I have no idea
what the choice even was every year someone's caught
spreading their loved one's ashes on the park ride
full of animatronic ghosts the decades grind on
like a millstone it's a great big beautiful tomorrow
sings the animatronic family while we clap along

Word of the Day

I've been sleeping well the queen died but not
of grief the new strip mall gun shop near campus
is called Trigger Therapy I don't think I'd want
to eat the rich I imagine noblesse oblige gives them
a slimy texture every day I get the feral mother
cat more acclimated to the live trap I've set out
on the patio where I feed her and her six kittens
while she eats food from my hand I can't help
feeling guilty for earning her trust just so I can
betray it I'm envious too of the way she closes
her eyes as she takes the food from my palm
not knowing that a single zip tie holds the trap
open my in-laws are in England the shops
are closed the museums full of looted antiquities
are closed the food banks are closed even cancer
patients can't get their infusions the queen died
but they won't die of grief they'll just die

Word of the Day

we scroll and swipe through endless byte-sized bites
that's what the AI suggests when I ask it to write
the opening line of a poem and hey I've seen
worse I can't help picking at the crack in the paint
on the bedroom wall I keep running a finger over
the slick flat place on my scalp where flesh was cut
away I keep thinking about the street where my father
lives avocado and grapefruit trees and the gentle
barking of the neighbors' dog down the hill but
at the end of the street just over the rise a sprawl
of refineries stretching all the way to the strait
as a kid I loved the glow of those refineries at night
drowsing in the back seat on our way somewhere
window cracked to the tang of estuary and sulfides
I ask the AI if poetry has value but I'm thinking
of how my father taught me to make decisions
flip a coin and while it's in the air ask yourself
what your heart wants it to land on I tell myself
if I keep clicking regenerate response the bot
will tell me what I want to hear on Saturday
mornings I make waffles shaped like Mickey Mouse
and all week long I keep telling my wife it's just
three more days until waffles it's just two more days

Word of the Day

I'm sitting on my wood deck trying to make friends
with the feral kittens in my yard when a snake
slides behind me just a slight pressure against my back
then its black gold red rings inches from my hand
as it slips down between the deck boards so OK
I stay pretty calm I'd been thinking about time
actually I was thinking about how I can draw
a line from my own mind back to my childhood
self but I don't think he would recognize himself
in me he was scared of pretty much everything
bright colors loud noises quiet noises cancer
other children the tiny gray men who definitely
lived in the furnace vent whereas I am only
frightened of calling strangers on the phone
and cancer but I was thinking if he could see
the adult he grew into that would just be one more
thing to be frightened of I've killed a few snakes
already the way my grandmother taught me
decapitation by garden hoe what would child me
think of that he couldn't bear to even look
at a drawing of a shark without getting woozy
anyway I chase the snake back into the bushes
away from the cats and tell myself there's nothing
to be afraid of this will all be OK this will be fine

Word of the Day

apparently airline pilots doze off midflight all the time
so what am I worried about really my colleague coughing
into her open hand at the colloquium sharks hurricanes
vending machines kill more people than sharks do
sometimes I wake up in a cold sweat remembering
the time a friend thought I'd forgotten her name I often
forget where I'm headed yesterday I drove halfway
to the grocery store before I remembered I was going
to work in 1958 the Air Force lost an atomic bomb off
the Georgia coast I can't keep straight which song
is Georgia on My Mind and which is Carolina in My
Mind though that should be easy Mike the Headless
Chicken lived for eighteen months after being decapitated
the farmer who failed to kill him fed him a mixture
of milk and water with an eyedropper over a year later
Mike choked to death in a motel room almost six hundred
miles from his home when people ask me where I'm from
I say I only live in Texas because I've never felt at home
here though I have lived in this house longer than any
other house in my lifetime when I wake up coughing
from a dream about being stabbed I read in the glow
of my phone a story about a man who thought he had
cancer and was shocked when surgeons removed
a five-centimeter living fir tree from his lung

Word of the Day

someone has spray-painted NO ICE CREAM FOR IAN
on the plywood boarding up the ice cream shop
hours before the hurricane fills the streets with
water with overturned cars with floating houses
in my yard a tree falls but another tree catches it
before it can cut my fence in half my mother texts
about how she almost fell down a flight of stairs
she sends a prayer-hands emoji a photo of the sewing
machine she dropped shattered on the landing
men in orange vests appear in my yard digging
holes looking for the sewer line break they give us
bottles of dye to pour down our drains but no
they can't find it they come back every day
for four days we do the same thing but no no no
someone keeps calling my number asking for Mark
no I say I don't know him the deer stand beside
the road as if waiting to throw themselves in front
of us as if to say didn't you build your house
in the floodplain didn't you climb that ladder
didn't you lean out over the balcony to take
a photo of a shark swimming down your street

Word of the Day

the billboard said the end of the world is coming
we pulled over and took a picture two years ago
I was writing a series in which I took a fragment
from Aeschylus and hid a rhyme of it inside
each poem but then a pandemic burned through
the country and I didn't write anything for a year
revising a poem I guess felt like washing my car
in the middle of a forest fire and we had plenty
of fires that year believe me that was the least
of it I know the odds that I'll win the lottery
are lower than the Mariana trench but the odds
someone will win aren't so bad and hey why not
me I got cancer again big deal my oncologist
said it was boring cancer the republic almost
ended big deal said the living smirk on cable TV
I kept a list of every terrible world-ending thing
and now looking over it I can't remember half
of them it's not very comforting to think of fire
as simply the transformation of matter from one
state into another especially when you're inside
the burning house apocalypse doesn't mean
the end it means uncovering like pulling back
the motel bedsheet to reveal the bugs already
crawling along the seams supposedly Aeschylus
died when an eagle mistook his bald head
for a rock and dropped a turtle on him
but somehow he's considered the father

of tragedy and not comedy ba dum bum
a million people died but big deal said
the ones who didn't this is not the sandwich
I ordered I want to speak to your manager
the next billboard said the end of the world
is here we drove past it we're still driving

3

Postoperative

Under the blanket, / under the gauze, / your stitches lined up / like immi-
grants / in dark coats, waiting / to enter one terrible / country after leaving /
another. Memories / fall away, one / by one, like ships going down / in a
storm, like a hundred little men falling off / a hundred little ladders. The
way hands held you / when you were the size / of an injured rabbit—gone. /
The cacti blooming / in your father's greenhouse, / the smell of new paint-
ings / hanging in your friend's apartment, / the trail through the woods
that led to a circle / of stones. Birds carry it all off. A shadow / falls over it. It
melts /on your tongue. But that loss / flies through you, / a sweet darkness.

Poem Not Ending with the President's Hands Upturned in an Expression of Unfathomable Indifference

At the restaurant, my wife frowns at her phone. A toddler is missing after her father made her stand outside at 3 a.m. as punishment for not drinking her milk. At least, that is what he tells reporters, a cavern in him where shame should be. A teenager flicks his smoldering cigarette into the brush below his parents' deck. Empathy's a kind of switch. On/off. Or the other kind, a branch for beating. This hurts me more, but that's just what one says, isn't it. No one being beaten ever feels sorry for the fist. It must be something. I know, I've done it. Turned up my hands. What can you do. What do you expect me to do about it. It is what it is. A wildfire erasing a city, a couple cowering in their swimming pool overnight, trying not to breathe too much smoke. You breathe too much, and that's it. Easier not to breathe. I work near the building where the state executes prisoners. Often, the executed have done monstrous things. Often, monstrous things were done to them. What can you do. Birds migrate across the ocean, their bodies shaped and weighted to make the trip. A storm diverts them. They get tired, fall into the sea, and drown. A hill shrugs several multimillion-dollar homes into the canyon below. The city releases the reservoir, floods the poorest neighborhoods. But to feel pity and call it empathy. Driving through downtown, I see the man with a bandaged foot tucked into the doorway of a church. Empathy's what I tell myself I feel, but that's a pill dissolving under my tongue. I feel your pain. But what are you going to do. But what can you do. It's almost like the whole world is wailing, calling out to me, and I have to carry around a card on which I've written a reminder: "I hear you."

74

Poem Not Ending with Anesthesia

I rode a gurney into the End Days, but the fine print I never
    read when I signed my name said, *We will move heaven*
    and earth to keep you alive so that you may go on signing our forms.

I've wept the way a gunman weeps as they carry him
in handcuffs past his dead.
          After we lost the election,
    they sent a dozen men in red caps to slash all the paintings
in the museum. They poured motor oil in the reservoir
    so they could charge more for beer.

          The man who all day
    removes ears with a box cutter understands both
terrors: our terror of pain, and our terror that we may
    survive that pain.

          In four years, I went under four times,
and that sleep was always sugar on my tongue. But to crack
    open a perfectly smooth egg and spill rotten yolk
down the bowl—how else can I describe recognizing

my own hands again, the disappointments of their function:
    to grasp, to make fists. Think
          of fanatics rubbing their raw eyes the morning after

the rapture fails to arrive. Or how the glove maker spends hours
    a day on a fine pair, lamb or peccary,
    only to see them on the tyrant's trembling
fists as he announces the latest pogrom.

I kept

a farmhouse like a bright coin in my pocket.

But when I returned there: the door stuck in its jamb,

the den stacked high with fascist literature, a room

I couldn't look at without imagining my grandfather dying on its floor

days earlier. When I'm dying for real, I will still tell myself

I might pull through this yet.

Oh but we walk the dark, preordained

to stumble, though didn't we lay each brick of the path

together?

When?

Some bright afternoon. Yesterday.

Yesterday is always yesterday.

But I remember that morning.

What happened?

Nothing. It was better. There was less

screaming.

No, the garden was always full of screams.

Ode to the Dead
of Bowling Green

—after the massacre

When I say ode, I mean shovel. When I say shovel,
I mean the horror movie heroine who opens the door
of the creaking shack. When I say dead, I mean hungry.
When I say hungry, I mean the student whose text alert
is the sound of a pistol cocking. When I say clock tower,
I mean the problem of evil—to wit, a man in a suit
who says immigrants but means slaves, a man in a suit
who says choice but means your children will barely
know how to read, a man in a suit who says compassion
and means let the elderly shut-ins starve. When I tell you
about three scars on my body, I mean there are more
scars than I can count. When I count, I mean that one
calamity should suffice. I can never say enough
but when I say enough, I mean we don't believe water
is wet until we're drowning. So when I say ode, I mean
its opposite. When I say hope, I mean the sound a torch
makes as it licks the books piled in the town square.

A Cloud Weighs
over a Million Pounds

And this was years after the cancer, still more
        since I sat on the floor
                of my college library
and read Forster: *the queen died, then the king died*

        is a story; *the queen died,*
                then the king died
of grief is a plot. At my friend's office,
        the motion-sensor lights
                        don't see her.

When she's typing and the room goes dark,
        she waves her arms
                like a shipwreck survivor.
How do I even begin? On Christmas Eve,

        I attended a children's play
                and when I came home,
I started shitting blood. There.   The saying goes:
        if you drop a frog
                in a boiling pot, he'll jump

right out. But if you put him
        in cool water
                and bring it slowly to boil, he'll submit
to being cooked alive.

[I do think there is blame—yes, I think there is blame on both sides. You look at, you look at both sides. I think there's blame on both sides, and I have no doubt about it, and you don't have any doubt about it either. And, and, and, and if you reported it accurately, you would say.]

The world is ending (again), and my options are:
 frowning face, face
    with single tear, face
of open-mouthed awe, laughing face, heart,

  thumbs up. Every day,
    I walk from my office
to the town square and back, and every day,
 I pass the stone marker
      IN MEMORY OF

       OUR

      CONFEDERATE

       PATRIOTS

   outside the courthouse. *What is*
the consistency? What is the frequency?

  Since I moved here,
    the state has executed
seventy-five prisoners in the red brick building
 a few blocks from my office.
    I don't want

to disappoint you, my friend says, *but the frog*
  will jump out
    the moment he gets uncomfortable.
What Forster meant: causality is key, but I missed

the point and studied
                grief instead. After days
of blood pouring out of me, I stopped eating. I
        deflated, hovered
                millimeters above

the floor. The cat's fur sparked
        at my fingertips.
                On the news, a story:
The child was placed in a detention center and later

        died. No, this was after
                the blood, after
my doctors' credentialed shrugs. I don't mean
        one thing caused
                the other. To be enormous

yet insubstantial yet feel a crushing weight,
        like the water
                that with every rain washes out
more of the flagstone path behind my house.

        Like my student who says,
                Nothing personal
after making another student cry. *Why are you
        getting so worked up?*
                When some people

in this country turn on the faucet, the water
        comes out
                flammable or full of lead or
the color of blood. I'd take it biblically

if I believed
        in any of that. *Can you estimate
the amount of blood?* asks the nurse in a way
        that tells me she's seen
                much worse.

I tell my friend she's living in a horror movie,
        that her building
                is plotting against her.
She tells me that a plot requires intent.

And sure, I'd prefer
        to believe
some liver-spotted oligarch tenting his fingers
        in the mahogany gloom
                of his office

meant it all to happen—the dead children,
        the blood, the plague
                of frogs. But terror is
mostly incremental and disjointed as the rain

that falls across the street
        while the sun shines
on my house, where I sit in my armchair
        watching a documentary:
                an insect walking

on water not by any miracle but by virtue
        of its insignificance.

Poem Not Ending
with My Grandfather's Will

The knife dulls a little
with every cut. There goes
grief, there goes sense.
There goes the squawking
flock of geese
above the dead girl's
house, and no one
will make the guilty kneel
on the cafeteria floor
to mop the blood
of children
with their neckties.
A piece of paper
says I own
the long, black case
fringed in padlocks
propped against
the closet wall. I'd rather
have the ladder
he climbed to pick apples,
but the dead teenager
doesn't get to pick the last
words she speaks
to her mother.
I don't want to hold it
again, as he taught me
when I was a child,
squinting down its length
at a milk jug full of sand
sitting on a stump

across the pasture.
But we like freedom,
we like choice,
we like atrocity
sensible and Midwestern,
five kinds of fruit salad
in the church basement
after the graveside service.

Photograph of My Wife
Shaving My Head

It's the dosage
that makes anything
poisonous, and poison,
in small quantities,
can cure you. How else to explain
that a waiting room can absorb
just some of the light
thudding through its windows,
and what we see is only the light each object
turns away? The plastic roses refuse
red. The nurse's nitrile glove
won't hold one blue photon.
The mountain snow
in the inspirational poster says no
to everything. How many times
did I wake, poison dripping into me,
my wife nearby in a chair
and in her lap the large green binder
in which she kept every schedule,
chart, prescription? Kindness,
in sufficient quantity, tastes
like mop bucket water. No? I didn't want
to believe it either, not even when I
cursed and knocked the cup
of ice chips to the floor.
Or the way I said thank you
to the nurse tugging staples
from my skin, thank you
to the nurse threading a tube
through a hole in my arm

all the way to my heart,
thank you to the nurse hanging
the bag of bleomycin. A little drop
of anger can cure your sadness,
and a little sadness can cure
your anger, but drink too deep—

How many times did I wake?
How many times did I thank pain,
or recoil from the cool palm
on my scalp? Love
enters the body
as through a cut
in the sole of the foot.
That's no secret.
But did you know
But did you know
But did you know

Mise en Abyme

In a diner in America, a child
colors in a placemat map of America,
all the jagged little states bursting
with color. She unwraps pats of butter, flattens
out the foil packages on which an Indian maiden
kneels, holding a box, on which an Indian maiden
kneels, holding a box, on which
you get the idea.

My friend the artist takes
a photo of herself in the mirror,
then has this photo tattooed
on her arm. Then she takes
another photo in the mirror,
showing off the tattoo
of her taking her photo
in the mirror.

And that box the Indian maiden
is holding is full of butter, which is full
of milk, which is full of grass,
which is full of sunlight,
which is full of subatomic quanta
that open like a set of matryoshka dolls,
each smaller than the last, forever.
Or the box is full of colonialism
pressed into golden bricks. Or the box
is empty. Or there is no box

because it is just a drawing
and not a box at all.

At night, my cat faces off
with her reflection in the patio door—
back arched, tongue on fire,
she raises her paw to strike it
but runs away when it raises a paw
to strike her back.

When all my hair had fallen out,
I stood naked in front of a mirror,
and the stranger on the other side
kept saying, "I'm you."
"I'm you," I repeated back
to him like a pet bird
imitating sounds
it can't understand:
tea kettle, game-show
theme song, a doorbell
ringing as the postman delivers a box
that contains a series of smaller
boxes, inside of which a tiny voice
chants, "I'm you, I'm you."

In the middle of an ocean, a continent.
Inside that continent, a great lake.
In the lake, an island.
On the island, a pond, and jutting above
the surface of its water, a rock.
I could go on.

The photo of my friend
showing off the tattoo
of herself taking a photo of herself hangs
in an art gallery, life-sized. I take a photo

of my life-sized friend standing beside it,
and then we walk out onto the street,
which is busy with traffic,
and enter a taxi in which a tiny toy taxi
hangs from the rearview mirror,
and inside it—maybe—a little us,
riding through the golden spiral of night.

The Survivorship

The corn shoots up every year
though we don't raise our eyes
from the breakfast table
long enough to notice.
It has always just sprouted
or is high as a tractor tire—all or nothing,
like the body and its nakedness.
But something must happen between
then and now. I remember Wooly Willy,
the cartoon man who smiled
from under plastic
while I rearranged his hair
and beard with a magnetic pen.
It was like that, decades
later—I wiped my hand
across my head, and the hair
came away like iron shavings.
In ancient Greece, *opiso* meant
both *future* and *behind*—the men
rowing the ships faced the ocean
they'd already traveled, not
the dark water still to come.
As I bit into my first caramel apple,
just over my shoulder
was my wedding, and while I slipped
the ring on my wife's finger,
standing behind me was a man in scrubs
holding a scalpel. Today I began

what my doctor calls *survivorship*,
and I saw an actual ship, wood
planks sealed with pitch against
the dark sea it cut through,
and when I turned to look behind me,
I couldn't tell water from water.

"Terrific," "Tremendous," "Loser," "Tough," "Smart," "Weak," "Dangerous," "Great," "Stupid," "Classy," "Big," "Huge," "Amazing," "Lightweight," "Win," "Bad," "Crooked," "Moron," "We," "They," "Zero"

Me, I like *susurrus*. I like *crepuscular, muscular, avuncular*. I like *aubergine, prokaryote, euphemism, portmanteau,* and *respite*. Don't get me wrong: I prefer *sea* over *ocean, woods* before *forest,* and I'll take *ache* over *agony*. I like *hasp* and *halyard* and *harpsichord*. I like *brood*. I like *tidy*. I crave *ruin* and *cleave* and *entropy*. I like both *cognate* and *false*. I like *measure* and *fathom*. I like *wherewithal* and *nonetheless*. True, I *hanker*. Yes, I *wallow*. I like *trepidation*. I *equivocate*. I *stall*. Oh, I *hem* and I *haw*. I *persevere*. I *profess*, I *protest*. I like how *just* requires one syllable and *unjust,* two. I like *brinkmanship* and *balkanize*. I like *reparation* and *repartee*. I like *depose*. I like how *cloud* feels heavy as *clod* and *schist* feels light as *wisp*. I like *calamity*. I like the way *witness* sounds—a knife drawn across a whetstone. I like *knife,* I like *whetstone*.

My Father, Singing

Yes, it's true: Americans can buy back the bombs
we dropped on Laos in the form of bangles
crafted from melted casings. This moment, three silver
circlets clink on the wrist of a woman
as she stretches to reach an apple
at the back of a bodega's fruit stand.
Beauty's built that way, but I don't mean
the hibiscus shampoo dripped
into a lab rat's eyes, or Elizabeth Báthory
climbing into a tub of virgin's blood. I don't mean
the woman at the bodega doesn't think
of someone else's child blown to bits
every time those bracelets jangle
down her arm. Maybe she does. I lived a year
beside a battlefield and didn't once lie awake
thinking of young men dying
in the pasture behind my house.
That was all ancient history, or near enough.
I made up metaphors about the cardinals
flitting by the window, though I know birdsong
is all struggle: draw the mate, warn
the rival. The egg hatches in a nest
of twisted reed and wire.
But when a tree sprouts
aboard the garbage barge
that's been circling
the ocean for years, it isn't proof

of anything. An uncle I never met
used to lock my father
in a room and beat him,
but I don't owe that uncle
for the way my father sang me to sleep
on the dark nights when I was afraid.

Poem Not Ending with a Transcript of the Final Voicemails of 9/11 Victims

Au clair de la lune, mon ami Pierrot, prête-m—
the earliest extant recording of a human voice,
its warble brushed into lampblack with pig bristle
(the tune a love song masquerading as a lullaby),
fourteen years before Alexander Graham Bell
turned a cadaver's ear into a recording device.
Someone told me once that *hearsay* came from
heresy, because gossip was a form of blasphemy,
but I only have his word to go on. The ear hears
the past: the workman hammering, his hammer
falling a heartbeat before the sound reaches
a boy watching the construction from behind
a fence. I close my eyes, and I'm a child
sitting on the floor, listening to the fan
in my mother's darkroom or the noise of my father
at his lathe in the basement. That's all Bell's
dead ear recorded: a whoosh, a blare, nothing
recognizable. My friend composes music played
on empty bowls. A bowl can only do what it does
because absence is part of its structure. Maybe
that's obvious. It holds broth, or assorted fruit,
or decorative glass beads, or, yes, a tone.
We know there's something unnatural about
taking a photograph (we say *taking* after all),
but it's sound that isn't meant to be held.
Flowers wilt, their stems cloud the vase
with slime, so we replace them with silk
and plastic, the water with blue glass beads.

Most footage of atomic bomb detonations
is dubbed with generic explosion noises.
The truth is loud and ugly and disappointing
and arrives thirty seconds after the bomb
goes off, the Joshua tree in the foreground
swaying slightly. Some of the canned laughter
played over the sitcoms you watched
as a kid was recorded decades earlier, and surely
some of those original audience members
were long dead but still laughing at bad
jokes—the root of *joke* originally meaning
to speak, to utter, or perhaps to confess,
though you didn't hear that from me.
Every sound is the completion of a promise—
the broken window, the unhappy child—
an acknowledgment that, yes, the pain
was real. Someone far off heard it and glanced up
from what they were doing and looked
all around to see where the sound came from.

An Urn for Ashes

The atoms that made up
Julius Caesar's body,
burned on a pyre,
spread by wind and time,
have since dispersed
far and wide,
and statistically speaking
you have in you
some infinitesimal bit
of carbon or hydrogen
from his hand or tongue,
or maybe some piece
of the foot that, crossing
a river, turned a republic
into an empire.
But that means you
carry with you also
the unnamed dead,
the serfs and farmers,
foot soldiers and clerks,
and their sandals
and the axles of chariots
and incense burned
at an altar and garbage
smoking in a pit outside
a great city at the center
of an empire, that you
are a vessel carrying
the ashes of many empires
and the ashes of people

burned away by empires,
their sweet, unheard melodies.
And look how finely wrought
you are, how precise
your features, your very form
a kind of ceremony
for transporting the dead
through the living world.

Acknowledgments

Many thanks to the editors of the journals that published some of these poems (sometimes in earlier forms and under different titles).

American Poetry Review: "Photograph of My Wife Shaving My Head," "Postoperative," "The Rabbit," and "Ruin"

Asphodel: The News from Poems: "Ode to the Dead of Bowling Green"

Bennington Review: "Word of the Day" [eating my sandwich outside . . .]

The Collagist: "Mise en Abyme"

Copper Nickel: "Poem Not Ending with a Transcript of the Final Voicemails of 9/11 Victims" (reprinted in the 2020 *Best American Poetry*) and "The Waffle House Index" (section vi from "After Aeschylus")

Gettysburg Review: "A Bow, a Basket, a Cloud" and "The Three Types of Knowledge"

Grist: A Journal of the Literary Arts: "The Survivorship"

Kenyon Review: "Poem Not Ending with U.S. Border Agents Tear-Gassing Migrant Children" and "'Terrific,' 'Tremendous,' 'Loser,' 'Tough,' 'Smart,' 'Weak,' 'Dangerous,' 'Great,' 'Stupid,' 'Classy,' 'Big,' 'Huge,' 'Amazing,' 'Lightweight,' 'Win,' 'Bad,' 'Crooked,' 'Moron,' 'We,' 'They,' 'Zero'"

NEA Writers Corner: "My Father, Singing"

Painted Bride Quarterly: "An Urn for Ashes"

Poetry Salzburg Review: "Poem on a Photo of a Reflection of a Bowl of Plastic Fruit"

Raleigh Review: "Word of the Day" [a truck carrying 100 monkeys . . .]

Sixth Finch: "Word of the Day" [as the roller coaster . . .], "Word of the Day" [I'm reading about . . .], and "Word of the Day" [the pollen falls . . .]

The Southern Review: "I Feel Like a Million $"

Sugar House Review: "Word of the Day" [the hosts of the true crime podcast . . .] and "Word of the Day" [I get emails all the time. . .]

Thanks also to Jesse Lee Kercheval, Cynthia Marie Hoffman, Shara Lessley, Quan Barry, John Lane, and Dona Lantz.

NICK LANTZ is the author of four previous books of poetry: *We Don't Know We Don't Know* (2010), *The Lightning That Strikes the Neighbors' House* (2010), *How to Dance as the Roof Caves In* (2014), and *You, Beast* (2017). His poetry has appeared in *American Poetry Review, Copper Nickel,* the *Gettysburg Review,* the *Southern Review,* and other journals, as well as in the *Best American Poetry* anthology. His poetry has received several awards, including the Larry Levis Reading Prize, the Great Lakes Colleges Association New Writer Award, and a grant from the National Endowment for the Arts. He teaches in the MFA program at Sam Houston State University and lives in Huntsville, Texas, with his wife and cats.

WISCONSIN POETRY SERIES

Sean Bishop and Jesse Lee Kercheval, *series editors*
Ronald Wallace, *founding series editor*

How the End First Showed (B) • D. M. Aderibigbe

New Jersey (B) • Betsy Andrews

Salt (B) • Renée Ashley

(At) Wrist (B) • Tacey M. Atsitty

Horizon Note (B) • Robin Behn

About Crows (FP) • Craig Blais

Mrs. Dumpty (FP) • Chana Bloch

Shopping, or The End of Time (FP) • Emily Bludworth de Barrios

The Declarable Future (4L) • Jennifer Boyden

The Mouths of Grazing Things (B) • Jennifer Boyden

Help Is on the Way (4L) • John Brehm

No Day at the Beach • John Brehm

Sea of Faith (B) • John Brehm

Reunion (FP) • Fleda Brown

Brief Landing on the Earth's Surface (B) • Juanita Brunk

Ejo: Poems, Rwanda, 1991–1994 (FP) • Derick Burleson

Grace Engine • Joshua Burton

The Roof of the Whale Poems (T) • Juan Calzadilla, translated by
     Katherine M. Hedeen and Olivia Lott

Jagged with Love (B) • Susanna Childress

Almost Nothing to Be Scared Of (4L) • David Clewell

The Low End of Higher Things • David Clewell

Now We're Getting Somewhere (FP) • David Clewell

Taken Somehow by Surprise (4L) • David Clewell

(B) = Winner of the Brittingham Prize in Poetry
(FP) = Winner of the Felix Pollak Prize in Poetry
(4L) = Winner of the Four Lakes Prize in Poetry
(T) = Winner of the Wisconsin Prize for Poetry in Translation

Thunderhead • Emily Rose Cole

Borrowed Dress (FP) • Cathy Colman

Host • Lisa Fay Coutley

Dear Terror, Dear Splendor • Melissa Crowe

Places/Everyone (B) • Jim Daniels

Show and Tell • Jim Daniels

Darkroom (B) • Jazzy Danziger

And Her Soul Out of Nothing (B) • Olena Kalytiak Davis

Afterlife (FP) • Michael Dhyne

My Favorite Tyrants (B) • Joanne Diaz

Midwhistle • Dante Di Stefano

Talking to Strangers (B) • Patricia Dobler

Alien Miss • Carlina Duan

The Golden Coin (4L) • Alan Feldman

Immortality (4L) • Alan Feldman

A Sail to Great Island (FP) • Alan Feldman

Psalms • Julia Fiedorczuk, translated by Bill Johnston

The Word We Used for It (B) • Max Garland

A Field Guide to the Heavens (B) • Frank X. Gaspar

The Royal Baker's Daughter (FP) • Barbara Goldberg

Fractures (FP) • Carlos Andrés Gómez

Gloss • Rebecca Hazelton

Funny (FP) • Jennifer Michael Hecht

Queen in Blue • Ambalila Hemsell

How to Kill a Goat & Other Monsters • Saúl Hernández

The Legend of Light (FP) • Bob Hicok

Sweet Ruin (B) • Tony Hoagland

Partially Excited States (FP) • Charles Hood

Ripe (FP) • Roy Jacobstein

Last Seen (FP) • Jacqueline Jones LaMon

Perigee (B) • Diane Kerr

American Parables (B) • Daniel Khalastchi

The Story of Your Obstinate Survival • Daniel Khalastchi

Saving the Young Men of Vienna (B) • David Kirby

Conditions of the Wounded • Anna Leigh Knowles

Ganbatte (FP) • Sarah Kortemeier

Falling Brick Kills Local Man (FP) • Mark Kraushaar

The End of Everything and Everything That Comes after That (4L) •
  Nick Lantz

The Lightning That Strikes the Neighbors' House (FP) • Nick Lantz

You, Beast (B) • Nick Lantz

The Explosive Expert's Wife • Shara Lessley

The Unbeliever (B) • Lisa Lewis

Radium Girl • Celeste Lipkes

Slow Joy (B) • Stephanie Marlis

Acts of Contortion (B) • Anna George Meek

Blood Aria • Christopher Nelson

Come Clean (FP) • Joshua Nguyen

Bardo (B) • Suzanne Paola

Meditations on Rising and Falling (B) • Philip Pardi

Old and New Testaments (B) • Lynn Powell

Season of the Second Thought (FP) • Lynn Powell

A Path between Houses (B) • Greg Rappleye

The Book of Hulga (FP) • Rita Mae Reese

Why Can't It Be Tenderness (FP) • Michelle Brittan Rosado

As If a Song Could Save You (4L) • Betsy Sholl

Don't Explain (FP) • Betsy Sholl

House of Sparrows: New and Selected Poems (4L) • Betsy Sholl

Late Psalm • Betsy Sholl

Otherwise Unseeable (4L) • Betsy Sholl

Blood Work (FP) • Matthew Siegel

Fruit (4L) • Bruce Snider

The Year We Studied Women (FP) • Bruce Snider

Bird Skin Coat (B) • Angela Sorby

The Sleeve Waves (FP) • Angela Sorby

If the House (B) • Molly Spencer

Wait (B) • Alison Stine

Hive (B) • Christina Stoddard

The Red Virgin: A Poem of Simone Weil (B) • Stephanie Strickland

The Room Where I Was Born (B) • Brian Teare

Fragments in Us: Recent and Earlier Poems (FP) • Dennis Trudell

Girl's Guide to Leaving • Laura Villareal

The Apollonia Poems (4L) • Judith Vollmer

Level Green (B) • Judith Vollmer

Reactor • Judith Vollmer

The Sound Boat: New and Selected Poems (4L) • Judith Vollmer

Voodoo Inverso (FP) • Mark Wagenaar

Hot Popsicles • Charles Harper Webb

Liver (FP) • Charles Harper Webb

The Blue Hour (B) • Jennifer Whitaker

American Sex Tape (B) • Jameka Williams

Centaur (B) • Greg Wrenn

Pocket Sundial (B) • Lisa Zeidner